THE

SUPERNOVAE, DARK ENERGY,

MYSTERIOUS

AND BLACK HOLES

UNIVERSE

"People want to know. Where did we come from? Where are we going? And when do we get there?"

—Robert P. Kirshner, *The Extravagant Universe*

THE

SUPERNOVAE, DARK ENERGY, AND BLACK HOLES

MYSTERIOUS

TEXT BY ELLEN JACKSON

PHOTOGRAPHS & ILLUSTRATIONS BY NIC BISHOP

Published in the United States by Sandpiper, an imprint of
Houghton Mifflin Harcourt Publishing Company. Originally
published in hardcover in the United States by Houghton
Mifflin, an imprint of Houghton Mifflin Harcourt Publishing
Company, 2008.

SANDPIPER and the SANDPIPER logo are trademarks of
Houghton Mifflin Harcourt Publishing Company.

For information about permission to reproduce
selections from this book, write to Permissions, Houghton
Mifflin Harcourt Publishing Company, 215 Park Avenue
South, New York, New York 10003.

www.hmhbooks.com

Book design by YAY! Design
The text of this book was set in Sabon.
The graph on page 47 was created by Jerry Malone.

The Library of Congress has cataloged the hardcover edition
as follows:
Jackson, Ellen B., 1943–
The mysterious universe : supernovae, dark energy,
and black holes / written by Ellen Jackson ;
photographs by Nic Bishop.
   p. cm. — (Scientists in the field)
Includes bibliographical references and index.
   1. Supernovae—Juvenile literature.
   2. Dark energy (Astronomy)—Juvenile literature.
   3. Black holes (Astronomy)—Juvenile literature.
   4. Astronomy—Juvenile literature.
   I. Title.

ISBN-13: 978-0-618-56325-8 hc
ISBN-13: 978-0-547-51992-0 pb

QB843.S95J33 2008
523.8'4465—dc22

2007041165

Printed in China / LEO 10 9 8 7 6 5 4 3 2 1
4500279378

SPECIAL THANKS TO

Alex Filippenko, professor of astronomy at the
University of California, Berkeley, who was ex-
traordinarily generous with his time and expertise
and did everything possible (and then some) to help
make this book a reality.

Alex Filippenko's research accomplishments,
documented in about five hundred published
articles, have been recognized with several major
awards, most recently the Richtmyer Memorial
Award (2007), and he is one of the world's most
frequently cited astronomers. His team's codiscov-
ery that the expansion of the universe is accelerating was voted the "Top Science Breakthrough of
1998" by *Science* magazine.

Dr. Filippenko has been voted the "Best
Professor on Campus" five times. In 2006, he was
honored as the Carnegie/CASE National Professor
of the Year among doctoral and research universi-
ties. He is the recipient of the 2004 Carl Sagan
Prize for Science Popularization.

CONTENTS

Please note that words italicized in the text are
defined in the glossary at the back of the book.

INTRODUCTION

You've probably heard that the universe is big. But do you have any idea just *how* big it is?

Chances are you're reading this book somewhere in North America on the planet Earth. But Earth is not the largest object in the solar system. Our sun is a star, a blazing fireball much, much larger than Earth. In fact, the sun is so huge that if it were a gumball machine, one million gumball-size Earths could fit inside it.

But some stars are enormous compared to our sun. Next to them, our sun would look like a small speck. Scientists have recently discovered three supergiant stars that could each hold more than a billion suns.

Even these stars are only tiny points of light in a larger group. On a clear, moonless night, if you lie on a grassy hillside far from the city lights and gaze upward, you'll see thousands of stars like pale fireflies winking against the silent dome of space. Most of these belong to our own Milky Way Galaxy, a vast island of gas, dust, and stars.

We can see only a part of the Milky Way Galaxy from Earth. But if you could go far, far out into space and look back, you would see a thrilling sight: an immense pinwheel of one hundred billion stars with a bulge in the middle. Our sun would be a tiny dot on the outskirts, like a house in the suburbs tucked away from the traffic jam in the city. If you could watch for 250 million years, you would see this mighty pinwheel turn once on its axis.

The Milky Way is not alone in the universe. In the 1920s, Edwin Hubble, the astronomer for whom the Hubble Space Telescope is named, discovered that a fuzzy patch in the sky was actually another galaxy very similar to our own. Astronomers soon noticed that this newfound galaxy, the Milky Way, and two or three dozen neighboring galaxies were all zooming through space in a group, like a galactic motorcycle gang.

And that's not all. Looking outward, astronomers have estimated that more than one hundred billion other galaxies, or clusters of galaxies, are strung across the visible universe like a lacy spider web. This web of galaxies is the largest structure known—an awesome spectacle at the threshold of our understanding. But like a web, it may be fragile and temporary. All these galaxies are in flight from one another, with the most distant galaxies racing away from the Milky Way at breathtaking speeds.

Our lives are short compared with the lives of the galaxies, which have been wheeling through space for billions of years. Like butterflies flitting among the ancient redwoods, we only catch a glimpse of these huge collections of stars frozen in time.

Although we can't see or feel it, everything in the universe is changing year by year, day by day. Some of these changes are slow and gradual; others are sudden and violent. The universe is filled with awesome power, mysterious energy, and mammoth explosions. It's truly worthy of our appreciation and wonder.

THINKING BIG

Big numbers can be difficult to imagine. If you wanted to count all the stars in our Milky Way Galaxy, how long would it take? If you never stopped to eat or sleep, it would take you more than one thousand years to count one hundred billion stars, counting three stars per second. But that's just the number of stars in *one* galaxy.

How many stars exist in the universe? According to Carl Sagan, a well-known astronomer, the total number of stars is greater than all the grains of sand on all the beaches of Earth combined.

Try to imagine sifting every grain of sand from every beach on Earth through your fingers. Scientists estimate that the total number of stars in the universe is greater than the number of all the grains of sand on our planet.

RIGHT

3

Supernovae have been described by ancient people throughout history. The most recent supernova in our own Milky Way Galaxy, Cassiopeia A (a Type II), occurred in 1680 and gave rise to the remnant shown in this photo. At its center is a neutron star.

A BLAST FROM THE PAST

Long, long ago and far, far away, a huge explosion rocked a distant *galaxy*. Tonight, billions of years later, a few tiny bits of light from that event have finally reached Earth, where they've just left a telltale trace on astronomer Alex Filippenko's monitor.

"Wahoo!" he shouts. "We nailed it. We've got a Type Ia (One-A) supernova!"

He jumps up and gives everyone a high-five. Alex is a whirlwind, full of energy and always on the go. Maybe that's why he studies *supernovae*, some of the greatest explosions in the universe.

This photo shows the remnant of Kepler's supernova, first observed by Johannes Kepler and others in 1604. At the time, the supernova appeared as a bright new star in the sky. Hundreds of years later, debris and gas from the explosion can still be seen.

Supernovae are stars—stars that die in an astounding blaze of glory. But these explosions are rare and very far away. Most stars, including our sun, won't end in a supernova explosion. In fact, no supernova has been observed in our galaxy for at least three hundred years. Scientists must turn their telescopes to distant galaxies and examine thousands at a time to find a few of these strange objects.

To most people, the stars that spangle the heavens seem eternal and unchanging. But supernovae are full of surprises, and the power behind them is almost impossible to imagine: some detonate with the energy of a billion, billion, billion hydrogen bombs.

Our sun is too small to become a supernova. Nevertheless, if it *could* become one, what would happen to our planet? Everyone and everything on Earth—the pyramids, the Grand Canyon, your friends and family—would be vaporized within minutes. As the shock wave moved outward, all the planets in the solar system would be blown to smithereens. Only a few fragments of debris and a huge cloud of gas would remain.

Surprisingly, from such a terrible event, great beauty is born. Thousands of years later, an astronomer on a distant planet might see a glowing shell of light in the night sky, the last trace of our sun and its planets.

"Supernovae are neat," says Alex. "But anyone who lives on a planet near a star that's about to explode should think about moving."

Alex and other astronomers want to learn everything they can about these amazing explosions. Supernovae are fascinating because they are so spectacular. There are also other reasons for Alex's interest.

Scientists think that most of the atoms in our bodies and everything around us, except for hydrogen, were formed in the hearts of stars and were spread throughout space by supernova explosions.

"If it weren't for supernovae, we wouldn't exist," says Alex. "The carbon in our cells, the oxygen that we breathe, the calcium in our bones—all were cooked up in the stars and expelled into space by these explosions."

The heat and pressure in stars fuse simple *atoms*, tiny particles of matter that make up everything we see, into other, more complex atoms. Without supernovae, these larger atoms, such as carbon and iron, would stay locked inside the stars forever. But when supernovae explode, they scatter these atoms throughout space.

Eventually the atoms created in supernovae swirl together like water in a whirlpool to form stars and planets, such as Earth. Carbon and other atoms come together to make up our bodies and the bodies of the plants and animals we see around us. Without supernovae, there would be no flowers or forests, no hummingbirds or humans.

Supernovae are also helping scientists understand a mystery that lurks in space. The discovery of a new substance called *dark energy* has stunned the scientific world. Until the 1990s, no one knew this strange energy existed. In fact, if you had asked a scientist about dark energy twenty years ago, you would have been told to stop watching so many science fiction movies. In contrast, today astronomers think it's very real.

Dark energy can't be seen, and that's why astronomers use the word *dark* to describe it. Like the wind, it's invisible. But supernovae and their galaxies provide a way for astronomers to detect dark energy.

Would you like to own a time machine? If the answer's yes, you might want to get a telescope. Telescopes show us what stars and galaxies looked like in the past.

The more distant an object, the longer its light must travel to reach Earth. If the sun went out right now, you could continue playing baseball for eight minutes before it became dark. This is the amount of time required for the sun's light to reach us.

Any star you see at night is much farther away than our sun. The star's light may have been traveling for hundreds of years, thousands of years, or even longer. For this reason, we don't see stars as they are; we see them as they were when their light left them. Some of the stars we see today may no longer even exist.

The supernovae Alex studies with the W. M. Keck Telescope in Hawaii may be in galaxies so far away that their light has traveled for billions of years to reach Earth. Many of the explosions he sees happened so long ago that Earth hadn't yet been formed when they went off. That's why every supernova is literally a blast from the past. And that's why looking through a telescope is like cruising through space—and time.

Scientists use the term *light-year* to measure distance to the stars. Light moves so fast that it can travel around Earth seven times in a second. The distance light travels in one year is 5.8 trillion miles or about 10 trillion kilometers. (That's a 1 followed by 13 zeroes!)

Nearby star (Vega): 27 light-years from Earth

Sun: 8 light-minutes from Earth

Supernova in a distant galaxy 8 billion light-years from Earth

Supernova in a nearby galaxy 250 million light-years from Earth

Moon: 1.3 light-seconds from Earth

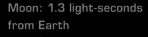

SPEED LIMIT 186,000 MPS

Not just a good idea, It's the law!

LEFT The time it takes for light to reach Earth depends on the distance of the light source. Light from nearby objects, such as the sun, reaches Earth fairly quickly. Light from a distant galaxy can take billions of years to make the journey.

Just as we can observe how the wind blowing the sails of a boat causes the boat to go faster, scientists can study dark energy by looking at objects, such as supernovae and their galaxies, and how they are affected by it.

Astronomers have known for decades that all the galaxies, including the ones that contain supernovae, are rushing away from one another. The universe itself is expanding or growing larger. But dark energy gives everything an extra push, and astronomers want to know what will happen to the universe in the future.

How do astronomers like Alex unlock these secrets of the universe? When people think of an astronomer, they may think of a lone figure, gazing at the glittering stars through the eyepiece of a telescope. In fact, modern astronomers such as Alex use computers to view the sky and seldom go near an eyepiece.

With the help of computers, Alex studies the brightest objects in the universe, supernovae, as well as the darkest objects, *black holes*, mysterious regions of space from which nothing—not even light—can escape. But that's not all he does. In addition to being an award-winning scientist, author, and lecturer, Alex is an outstanding teacher, who twirls doughnuts on strings or leaps on tables to demonstrate a point. At the University of California, Berkeley, where Alex teaches, students have voted him "Best Professor on Campus" five times.

"He's so enthusiastic, it rubs off on you," says Mohan Ganeshalingam, one of Alex's graduate students. "After talking to Alex, I walk away feeling that this is the greatest stuff in the world. Everyone should be an astronomer."

Alex has won many awards for his teaching and research. He uses music, balls, doughnuts, and even T-shirt diagrams to help explain astronomical ideas to his students.

Alex often brings students with him when he travels to the Keck observatory in Hawaii to view supernovae. Tonight, in the control room, Alex is accompanied by Ryan Foley, a graduate student who's assisting him with his research.

The twin Keck telescopes sit atop Mauna Kea, an inactive volcano. Rising 13,796 feet (4,205 meters) above sea level, Mauna Kea is higher than nine Empire State Buildings stacked on top of one another. At the summit, the city lights are almost invisible, the air is clear and dry, and most of the clouds float far below. You won't find a better view of the starry skies. At such a high altitude, however, some people get dizzy and confused from lack of oxygen. And an astronomer who's confused might add when he should subtract, or mistake a star for a galaxy.

Joel, the telescope operator who's controlling the telescope tonight, must stay at the summit to do his work. Because he's on duty for several days, Joel has had time to adapt to the altitude. But most astronomers prefer to work closer to sea level, and thanks to modern technology, they can. Fiber-optic cables link the actual telescope on Mauna Kea to the telescope control room far down the mountain in the town of Waimea.

And that's where Alex and Ryan are working tonight. In the Waimea control room, several computer workstations sit on tables, and two whiteboards hang on the walls. Joel can be seen on one screen; a small video camera allows him to look back at Alex and Ryan.

A notice on one of the whiteboards tells Alex and Ryan when the local coffee shop closes. Astronomers often chow down on fast food while they're working at Keck because they don't want to waste precious time. Building, operating, and maintaining a telescope such as the Keck is expensive. The cost, averaged out over the lifetime of the telescope, comes to a dollar a second, or $40,000 a night. Unfortunately, this amount is the same whether astronomers get useful results or not.

The two Keck telescopes are in high demand among astronomers. The 33-foot (10-meter) Keck telescopes can look backward into the most distant past and analyze the faintest objects in the universe. For this reason, more than one thousand astronomers apply to use the Kecks each year, but only about half get that privilege.

The project Alex and Ryan are working on is considered high priority, and Alex has no difficulty getting telescope time. He's part of the High-Z Supernova Search Team, a group of approximately twenty astronomers in one of two teams that originally discovered dark energy. Their goal is to figure out how dark energy interacts with normal matter and to understand its importance in the universe.

Dark energy is important because scientific knowledge is like a pyramid. If one of the blocks at the bottom of the pyramid turns out to be made of Jell-O, the whole structure is in danger of falling. In this case, one of the building blocks of the universe has turned out to be dark energy. And astronomers need to learn more about this new "substance" that makes up a large chunk of the universe.

To unlock the mysteries of dark energy they must study the light from a wide range of supernovae. That means observing with the Keck so they can study the most distant objects. For now,

Light from a star or a light bulb looks white, but it can be separated into many different colors, forming a *spectrum*. The dark absorption lines in this spectrum are like fingerprints that indicate the presence of certain atoms or elements, such as hydrogen, calcium, or sulfur.

COLOR CODED

Alex and Ryan use a special instrument called a spectrograph to study supernovae. The spectrograph breaks the supernova's light into its different colors the way a prism breaks light into a rainbow.

Nearly everything astronomers know about stars and supernovae comes from studying their light. The intensity of red, blue, green, or yellow light tells them how hot the object is; blue objects are much hotter than red objects. Dark and bright lines at certain locations in the star's spectrum will reveal what kinds of atoms or *elements* (such as calcium, sulfur, and silicon) the star contains, how big the star is, and how fast it's moving (or was moving when the light left it). Astronomers look for these lines to learn what kind of object they're observing.

Alex and Ryan must decide which object from their list they should target next.

"I like K467 because it's not in a bright galaxy," says Alex. Every supernova is in or near a galaxy, but too much light from the surrounding stars can spoil the data from the supernova.

"I don't like that one," notes Ryan. He suggests K439, which he thinks is more likely to be a normal Type Ia supernova. The problem is that K439 sits directly in a bright galaxy, so it won't provide as good a *spectrum* (see sidebar). Alex will make the final decision.

People sometimes have difficulty understanding how the universe can be expanding. Imagine a chocolate chip cake baking in the oven. As the cake rises, it gets larger. Each of the chocolate chips inside the cake moves away from every other chocolate chip. This is similar to the way the galaxies all move away from each other. But unlike the cake, the universe has no edges, no bottom, and no top. And it doesn't just fill your oven, it fills everything!

If the universe is expanding, what is it expanding into? The extra distance isn't really coming from anywhere. More and more space is coming into existence as the universe ages. Yet the universe itself has no boundaries, and some astronomers think it may be expanding into another dimension, a part of space we can't see.

Every object in the universe attracts every other object, and this attraction is

Alex demonstrates the expansion of the universe with Ping-Pong balls on a bungee cord. As the cord is stretched, the Ping-Pong galaxies move farther apart. In a similar fashion, as the universe expands, every galaxy moves away from every other galaxy. The galaxies and galaxy clusters stay the same size as the space between them increases.

called *gravity*. For a long time, astronomers thought that the expansion of the universe must be slowing down because of gravity. At this very moment, you are experiencing Earth's gravity, the force that holds your feet on the ground so that you don't float off into space. Strictly speaking, both you and Earth have gravity. But Earth is much more massive—that is, it is made up of more material—and its gravity is much stronger than yours.

When you fire a cannonball into the distance, it will eventually fall to Earth. In the same way, astronomers believed that the gravity of all the galaxies together would slow the universe's expansion.

If you saw a ball rolling down the street, you might wonder: did someone give that ball a kick? Or does the street slope slightly so that the ball is rolling downhill and gaining speed as it goes? If you were a scientist, you might take some measurements to find out if the ball is rolling faster and faster, maintaining the same speed, or slowing down a bit. Such observations would hint at what started it rolling in the first place and what kinds of forces are affecting its motion.

Likewise, in the 1990s, astronomers like Alex began to make precise measurements of supernovae. They measured the speed of both distant and nearby supernovae to see how fast they were moving in the present compared with how fast they had been moving in the past. Piece by piece, they began to put the puzzle together. Soon, they believed, they would know just how much gravity was putting the brakes on the universe and slowing its expansion.

But dark energy was about to enter the picture. The astronomers were in for a surprise.

A supernova shock wave hits a region of dense gas, heating it up and causing it to glow.

PINPRICKS OF LIGHT

Alex liked science even as a child. He once found a female spider and brought her inside, hiding her under the stairs. Soon the house was full of baby spiders. He brought magnets to school and played with them for hours, dragging them through the sand in the sandbox to pick up iron filings.

But the school counselor didn't recognize him as a budding scientist. She thought Alex spent too much time with the magnets, instead of with other children.

"I don't know why she was concerned," says Alex. "I had friends. We used to play Red Rover together. I was really good at it." Then he adds with a smile, "She also thought I ate too many peanut butter and jelly sandwiches."

More than anything, though, Alex liked to play with chemistry sets. This interest lasted into his teenage years. And because he was a model student, he was allowed to use the chemistry lab after school.

One day, he was squishing some explosive chemicals together when they suddenly blew up in his face. He lost an eyebrow and some hair, but nobody found out what he'd been up to.

Another time, he decided to mix up a substance contained in fireworks. Again, the mixture exploded in his face. This time the lab supervisor noticed a cluster of purple beads splattered on the ceiling, and Alex had to confess.

When Alex was fourteen, his parents bought him a small telescope for Christmas. He set up the telescope and pointed it at a bright object in the sky. The object came into focus, and Alex realized it had tiny rings. He was looking at a planet.

"I discovered Saturn that night," explains Alex.

"It didn't matter that people before me had seen it. Not only was it beautiful; it showed me the feelings people can get from making a discovery. And then I thought, *If I can get so excited about finding something millions of people have seen before, how great it would be to discover something in nature no one else knows about.*"

In high school, he joined a local astronomy club and helped arrange star parties, gatherings at which members set up their telescopes for the purpose of sharing their knowledge of the sky with the public. But after Alex and his older brother watched a television documentary about an astronomer, he wasn't sure he wanted to be one.

"They showed the astronomer sleeping all day and then going to the dome and looking through an eyepiece all night," he says. "The astronomer didn't interact with people much. It looked like he was some kind of mole."

In college Alex first majored in chemistry, a science that deals with the behavior of atoms and molecules, the tiny particles of matter that make up everything we see. Then later he switched to physics, specifically astrophysics, when he realized that as an astronomer he could study chemistry and also the behavior of the really *big* objects in the universe.

"I wanted to study the universe on the smallest and largest scales," he says.

Today, Alex has a busy life. Not only does he work as part of a team, but he co-writes at least twenty papers a year and frequently lectures to the public. Along with his work in the classroom, he's taught three astronomy video courses and co-written a popular astronomy textbook. He also spends many hours reviewing other scientists' papers and applying for funding and telescope time for various projects.

In his free time, Alex is an enthusiastic tennis

In Hawaii, Alex takes time out to do some boogie boarding.

player and hiker. And he likes to travel, especially if he can go somewhere interesting to view a total solar eclipse. Alex also enjoys spending time with his wife and three children.

"The truth is, you're only a mole if you want to be," says Alex. "But I take on way too much, and I've never learned how to say no."

Despite his busy schedule, Alex likes to share the excitement of science with others. In fact, it's not unusual for Alex to talk about science with students for three hours at a time over pizza. One of the students invited to Alex's pizza lunches a few years ago was a fifteen-year-old high school student, Harrison Pugh. Harrison became fascinated by astronomy and was allowed to take Alex's astronomy class at UC Berkeley even though he was younger than the other students. Alex invited him to become a supernova checker, and Harrison eventually discovered a number of supernovae on his own.

Harrison isn't the only student who has experienced the thrill of working with Alex. Each year, Alex holds a contest asking students to express why they'd like to win an all-expenses-paid visit to Lick Observatory for a night to help conduct research. Humor is encouraged. One student brought his band and played the Beatles' song "Here Comes the Sun" for Alex. Another student wrote an essay on poster board. She pasted astronomically named candy (Mars, Milky Way, Orbit, Starburst) throughout the essay in special places. Another did the hula.

Alex has other ways to keep his students interested. He often uses props in his class, throwing balls and blowing up balloons to make science come alive. On Halloween he dresses up as a black hole—a black hole that radiates candy instead of energy.

Alex dressed as a black hole. The little spaceman around his neck has been captured by the hole's gravity.

"Alex does some pretty crazy stuff in his astronomy class," says a student. "A few years ago, he was doing a demo. He was trying to show how electrons in atoms jump between different energy states. So he jumped from the chair to the table and back to the chair again. The chair broke and Alex cracked a rib. Astronomy is a dangerous field."

THE KECK TELESCOPE CONTROL ROOM (WAIMEA, HAWAII)

Alex has decided he and Ryan will make observations of both objects K467 and K439, but only for thirty minutes each. Before the night began, Alex sent a file to Joel, the telescope operator. The file contains a list of all the possible objects Alex might want to observe, along with their positions. Now he tells Joel to point the telescope at K439.

First, Joel finds a *guide star*, a bright star near the object that can be used to guide the telescope to the correct part of the sky. He moves the telescope again and adjusts it until he has the object in position. Then the precious *photons*, or bits of light, light that's been traveling for billions of years, can be collected. This process can be difficult because some of the objects are so far away or so dim, they can't be seen on the monitor. There's always a chance Alex and Ryan might be taking pictures of empty space.

Alex gets information about the location of each object from other members of his High-Z Supernova Search Team who have been working in South America. For this project, they have been allotted telescope time on the 13-foot (4-meter) Blanco telescope in Chile. The Blanco has a large camera, so it can take a picture of a wide area of sky in a single shot. Then, with the help of computers, the astronomers compare the newest pictures of galaxies with older pictures of the same galaxies taken a month earlier. Images with new

DINOSAURS AND SCOOBY-DOO

Astronomers all over the world are busy looking for supernovae, and they need to keep track of the ones they find. Supernovae discoveries are reported to the International Astronomical Union, and each is given an official name.

The first part of the name is a number designating the year the supernova was discovered. The first twenty-six supernovae of the year are given a capital letter from A to Z: 2006F, 2007S, and so on. When the capital letters are used up, pairs of lowercase letters are used: aa, ab, ac . . . bd, be, bf, and so on. Several hundred supernovae a year are discovered by both professional astronomers and amateurs.

Alex and his team have their own system of naming and numbering. Some of the objects their telescopes identify may not be true supernovae. So until the objects are officially classified, they are given a letter that designates the month in which they were discovered and a number that gives the order of discovery. Using this system, Alex can tell immediately that K439 was discovered earlier in the month than K467.

But astronomers also like to give supernovae fun names, too, just to use among themselves. Supernovae have been named after superheroes, cartoon characters, and even dinosaurs.

"One was named Bullwinkle and one was Scooby-Doo," Alex explains. "Dudley Do-Right once made it into a paper. At the time, he was one of the most distant supernovae we'd found."

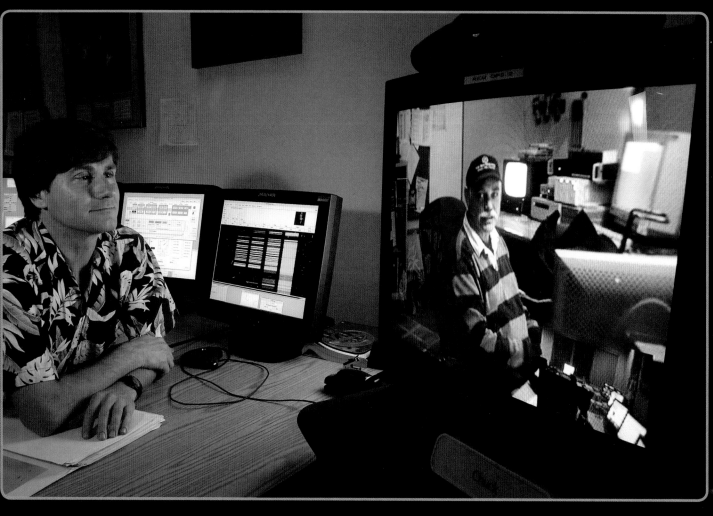

While he works from the Waimea control room, Alex can see and talk to the telescope operator, who stays at the summit of Mauna Kea and points the telescope at the objects Alex and Ryan want to study. Chuck Sorensen, one of the operators, is visible on the screen.

Almost every speck of light in this photo, taken by the Hubble telescope, is a galaxy similar to our own. Galaxies such as these, each containing billions of stars, appear everywhere in space as far as astronomers can see.

RIGHT

points of light that might be supernovae are flagged.

The Blanco telescope can examine one hundred thousand galaxies a night. It's a little like panning for gold and looking for a few sparkling flecks among all those grains of sand. Every five minutes, the Blanco sweeps a small patch of sky, about the size of the full moon as it appears from Earth, looking for the one galaxy out of thousands that contains a supernova.

Imagine that the night sky is a black dome rotating above your head with billions of tiny pinpricks punched in it to represent all the galaxies that our telescopes can see. Now imagine that the moon is a golden sticker pasted on the dome. Peel off the sticker. How many galaxies will you find under it? This is the answer: five hundred thousand. That's how many galaxies are there, although the Blanco, with its short exposure time, can detect only five thousand of those.

Amazing as it seems, a small moon-size patch of sky, even a patch that looks dark, is awash with half a million pinpricks of light, each one a galaxy. And each of those galaxies is composed of hundreds of billions of finer pinpricks—stars. But the individual stars in each galaxy can't be detected, even with the strongest telescope, unless one of them explodes and becomes a supernova.

The odds are good that a number of supernovae, perhaps ten, can be found with the Blanco before the night's over. It still isn't certain that all of these objects are supernovae, but they are all possibilities. The list is sent to Alex, who chooses the most likely candidates to check out more closely with the Keck.

"We've got the object," says Alex. He begins the exposure. "We'll know what it is in thirty minutes."

The W. M. Keck Observatory is home to two of the largest optical telescopes in the world. The third object (on the left) in this photo is the Subaru telescope, owned and operated by Japan. The photo shows the three telescopes at sunset, high above the clouds.

TWO DAZZLING DOMES

Once they've got the telescope in position, Alex and Ryan have to wait anywhere from twenty minutes to an hour for enough light to arrive at the telescope to give them a good spectrum of the object. The spectrum, which is displayed as a graph, will help them figure out what the object is. If Alex and Ryan have guessed wrong and the object isn't a supernova, especially the kind they're looking for, a Type Ia, they've wasted valuable time.

The Crab Nebula is the remnant of a Type II supernova explosion in the Milky Way Galaxy. Chinese, Japanese, Korean, and Arab astronomers recorded this supernova in 1054. The Chinese referred to it as a "guest star." The photo was created by combining optical, infrared, and x-ray images.

It's easy for a scientist to get things wrong when he's searching for supernovae. Stars can explode in different ways, and it's important for Alex to know what kind of object he is looking at.

Supernovae come in two main varieties: Type I and Type II. Type I supernovae are further divided into a number of different subtypes, Type Ia, Type Ib, Type Ic, and so on.

Type II supernovae are caused by the explosion of very big stars. The bigger, more massive stars—those more than eight or ten times as large as the sun—enjoy an exciting life with plenty of fast living. They burn brightly for a few million years and then come to a violent end as supernovae.

After exploding, a Type II supernova can leave behind a strange object called a *neutron star*. Normal stars are made of ordinary atoms composed of a nucleus with electrons zipping around at a distance. In a neutron star, those atoms have been squashed together by gravity so tightly that the whole star is like one big, heavy, and very dense atomic nucleus. A teaspoon of material from a neutron star would weigh more than a pile of a billion cars.

Smaller stars, such as our sun, seem like dim bulbs in comparison. Most will burn steadily for billions of years, and then end their lives as small, dense *white dwarfs*, eventually fading away. Ho hum! What a boring life.

This illustration
shows the comparative sizes
of a white dwarf (left),
a neutron star
(the dot in the middle),
and the planet Earth (right).
The white dwarf
is extremely dense
and weighs as much as
300,000 Earths. Despite its
tiny size, the neutron star
has even greater
density, weighing as much as
500,000 Earths.

In this photo, Supernova 1994D can be seen on the outskirts of galaxy NGC 4526. This supernova has been identified as a Type Ia.

But not every white dwarf simply fades away. A special few, those that are located near a larger star, go out with a bang and become Type Ia supernovae. This is the type of supernova Alex and his team are studying tonight.

All Type Ia supernovae explode when they grow to be the same size: about 1.4 times the *mass* of our sun. And all Type Ia supernovae blaze with the power of billions of suns. In fact, they're so bright they can be seen across the universe, which makes them useful as *standard candles*.

Every Ia begins with a pair of stars located very close to each other. The two stars revolve around each other like dancing partners. One star is a small, dense white dwarf and the other is probably a

much larger star, although scientists are less certain about this theory. The white dwarf is something of a thief, since it steals material from the other star and gets away with it, at least for a while. How does it do this? The white dwarf pulls material from the other star with its gravity. This process continues until the white dwarf reaches the critical mass and becomes unstable. KABOOM! It explodes in a mind-boggling supernova blast.

Is Alex looking at a Type Ia supernova or something else? Even Type Ia supernovae can differ from each other in small ways, just as the fingerprints of identical twins are not exactly alike. It's important that astronomers understand all the differences in order to figure out which elements are produced at every stage of the explosive process.

Alex tries to measure the entire *light curve*—the increase in light, the peak, and then the decrease—over a period of about a month. The bigger and brighter supernovae rise and fall at a slower rate than the dimmer ones. Observing the entire curve helps

Ryan checks a spectrum on a computer monitor.

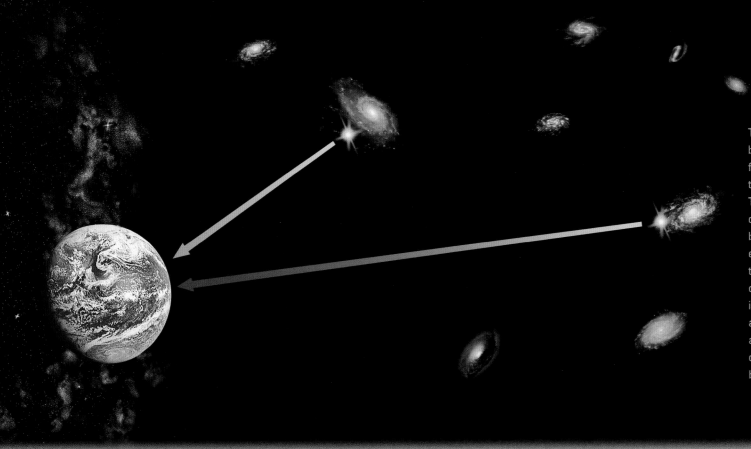

Type Ia supernovae are the best "standard candles" for measuring the distance to far-off galaxies. A Type Ia supernova is an object that has a known brightness. Just as an earthbound observer can tell how far away a distant car is by noting how bright its headlights seem, astronomers can estimate a Type Ia supernova's distance by looking at how bright it appears.

STANDARD CANDLES

Finding an accurate way to measure distances has always been a problem for astronomers. How do you tell the difference between a distant bright galaxy and a dim galaxy that's much closer? They both might look exactly the same in the sky.

If you see a car's headlights from far away, you can estimate its distance because you've seen car headlights up close and you know how bright they are. If the headlights appear very dim, you know the car is far away.

Type Ia supernovae work the same way. They're all about the same size and brightness, just like 100-watt light bulbs. If Alex sees a Type Ia supernova that looks quite dim, he knows it's distant—and so is its galaxy.

It's as if each Type Ia supernova wears a sign that says: "I'm dim because I'm eight billion light-years away." Another sign might say: "I'm bright because I'm only one billion light-years away."

Type Ia supernovae are the only objects in the universe that can serve as mileage markers. Normal stars can't do it. Why? Stars can't be seen when they're far away because they just

aren't bright enough. Also, stars come in different sizes; some are huge, but others are really tiny and faint. Galaxies have the same problem.

But by knowing how far away each Type Ia is, Alex and Ryan can read its spectrum and find out how fast the supernova and its galaxy were moving when the supernova exploded. Remember, we are looking into the past when we look at distant objects. By analyzing many Type Ia supernovae, astronomers can tell if these objects were getting an extra push from dark energy at the time they went off.

The dense white dwarf in this illustration attracts matter from a larger companion star. The added matter causes the white dwarf to grow in mass and makes its temperature rise.

Alex identify what type of supernova he's seeing with a greater degree of certainty.

"Let's say you know you're looking at headlights, but you have no idea what type of headlight you're seeing," explains Alex. "You have bicycle headlights, car headlights, and big semi-tractor-trailer truck headlights. If you just made a head-light measurement and got a distance and didn't even consider that there might be differences, you could easily get the wrong answer—"

Ryan interrupts him. The moment of truth has arrived. The results are in for supernova K439, but they aren't clear.

"I wouldn't bet my cat on this one," says Alex. "I'd call it a supernova, but is it a Type Ia? We really can't tell."

When the white dwarf grows to about 1.4 times the mass of the sun, it becomes unstable. The end result is a Type Ia supernova explosion. The supernova in this illustration has just started to explode and is blowing some of the companion star's gases away from it.

At almost 13,796 feet (4,205 meters) the summit of Mauna Kea is above 40 percent of Earth's atmosphere. The thin, clear mountain air allows the Keck telescopes to see far into space with great clarity.

MAUNA KEA

It's the following day and Alex decides to drive to the summit of Mauna Kea. The uncertain results from last night have made him wonder if one of the optical instruments might be dirty or smudged. It's an excuse to visit the telescope, and Alex likes to do that whenever he can.

He drives past lava fields, grasslands, and grazing cattle, and soon the road becomes rough and winding with hairpin turns. Signs warn of steep grades and wandering cows. As Alex approaches the summit, the vista becomes a barren moonscape of rust-colored rocks; in fact, the terrain is so much like the moon that the Apollo astronauts trained here in the 1960s.

At the summit, the dazzling white domes of Keck I and Keck II appear. The two telescopes share the mountain with a dozen other domes and dishes, but they're the most well known. When scientists began looking for a place to put the world's largest telescope, they could find nowhere better than Mauna Kea. Other mountains were higher, but none had such calm weather at the summit and dark skies.

The first Keck telescope began observations in 1993. But Alex was interested in telescopes long before the Kecks were built. And he's come when he scanned the heavens with a beginner's telescope.

Now he works with two of the most amazing instruments on Earth. The Keck I and Keck II stand eight stories high and weigh 300 tons apiece. Each telescope has thirty-six segments that work together as if they were one large 33-foot (10-meter) mirror, a mirror with an ability to detect objects four times fainter than those that can be seen by the 200-inch (5-meter) Hale telescope on Mount Palomar, California.

When we see a bright object from Earth's surface, the movement of the air overhead makes the object flicker, or twinkle. Twinkling may be great for nursery rhymes, but it's bad for astronomers. The Keck telescopes have been built on Mauna Kea above 40 percent of Earth's atmosphere to get away from dirt, smog, and twinkle.

Recent advances have further reduced this twinkling. Each of the two telescopes comes equipped with a flexible mirror about the size of a Frisbee. These additional mirrors flex just enough to correct for any distortion caused by the moving atmosphere, and they do it 670 times a second. They help the Keck images stay as crisp and clear as those taken from outer space.

Alex crunches his way across the broken lava of Mauna Kea. It's icy cold with an average temperature of 30 degrees Fahrenheit or –1 degree Celsius. There's no vegetation, just every possible color and shape of lava. Hawaiian lava comes in two varieties: one that's smooth and easy to walk on and another that's spiky, sharp, and dangerous, called 'a'a (pronounced "ah-ah"). If you fall on it,

you'll know where it got its name.

Only a few creatures manage to live at the summit: the occasional centipede, hunting spider, moth, and weiku bug. If you pick up a weiku bug, the warmth of your hand will kill it.

Alex punches in a security code and enters the observatory. He passes the main computer area and heads for a small room that holds spare mirrors for the telescope. All is in good working order.

Next Alex enters the dome, a hollow hulk of steel beams and gears. He climbs to a catwalk and talks with one of the technicians. At night, visitors can feel a faint rumbling when the dome turns and the shutters open so the telescope can be pointed toward an object of interest. But at the moment, everything's quiet.

The air inside the dome is chilly, and Alex keeps his jacket on. It costs $35,000 a month just to keep the inside of the Keck domes near freezing so that changes in temperature won't distort the mirrors or other metal equipment.

The technician and Alex examine a slit mask, a piece of aluminum with a number of slits cut into it. Before an observing run, astronomers write a program describing what they want to see in the sky. The technicians use the program to build a mask using a machine that cuts metal. Later, the mask is inserted into the spectrograph. Each slit, or hole, on the mask is positioned to allow only the light from the target objects to come through. Everything else is blocked out.

Astronomers like Alex spend a lot of time checking their equipment. Because the objects he studies are so distant and so faint, all kinds of things can go wrong. The slits might be in

The interior of the Keck dome is so vast that the photographer has had to create a composite picture, using many photographs. The telescope's huge (33-foot/10-meter diameter) mirror can be seen.

the wrong place, the edges of the slits might be too rough, or there might be debris on the mask.

A telescope is like a light bucket, designed to detect the tiniest trace of light. That's why astronomers search for supernovae only when the moon is below the horizon and the sky is dark. Unfortunately, a few wandering photons from the city lights below or a speck of dust can ruin a night's work.

The night sky may appear dark to you, but it's actually glowing with light from homes, shopping centers, and other sources. Air, dust, and water vapor reflect much of the light back toward Earth, where it becomes a problem for astronomers.

When things are functioning well, only light from a star or supernova is gathered by the Keck and sent to a camera with a light-sensitive computer chip, called a charge-coupled device (CCD). The CCD is covered with millions of tiny squares, or pixels. When the light hits one of the pixels, a signal is sent to a computer.

The computer collects the signals from all the pixels to form an image of the object. A CCD camera is great for showing close-ups, but it can cover only one small piece of the sky at a time.

"The objects we're looking at are one hundred times fainter than the night sky," says Alex. "The stars are all up during the day. People don't see them because of the brightness of the sky. But even at night, extra light can drown out our signal.

"Sometimes it's good just to take a look at the instruments," Alex continues. "Dust and other stuff settles on them. If we can't find the objects we're looking for, we're dead in the water."

The slit or hole in the mask allows only the light from the target object to come through. The holes are elongated because the observed object moves across the sky as Earth rotates.

Notice how the dark absorption lines appear to move toward the red end of the spectrum when an object is moving away from Earth. As astronomers look out farther into space, they see greater and greater degrees of redshift.

DARKNESS EVERYWHERE

E dwin Hubble was the first astronomer to discover that the universe is expanding. When he measured the *redshift* of distant galaxies, he discovered that every galaxy was moving away from every other galaxy.

RED SHIFT, BLUE SHIFT

When astronomers want to know how fast something is moving, they measure its redshift. We've all heard a fire engine go by with its siren blaring. If you listen carefully, you'll notice that the pitch of the siren rises as the fire engine approaches you. Then it drops when the fire engine moves away. This change in pitch is called the *Doppler effect*.

Light behaves in a similar way. But instead of the pitch changing, the color of light changes by a tiny amount. If the source of the light is moving toward you, the light shifts toward the blue end of the spectrum. That's because the waves of light are squeezed or bunched together. If the source is moving away, the light is stretched out and the color shifts toward the red end of the spectrum.

When scientists look at light from a star or supernova, lines in the spectrum show what it's made of. The amount of the redshift or blueshift tells them how fast the object is moving. Almost all distant objects have a high redshift because the expansion of the universe is carrying them away from Earth. Astronomers indicate the amount of redshift by using the letter *z*. That's why Alex's group, led by Brian Schmidt of the Australian National University, is called the "High-Z Supernova Search Team." They're looking for highly redshifted, and therefore very distant, supernovae.

Astronomers reasoned that if the galaxies are growing farther apart, they must have been much closer together in the past. But what started the expansion?

Most astronomers think a giant explosion, called the *big bang,* gave birth to our universe about 13.7 billion years ago. That explosion is still driving the expansion we see around us.

With the big bang, time, space, and all matter came into existence. In a fraction of a second, the universe unfurled from a point smaller than an atom and became a blazing ball of bright light. It grew to the size of a galaxy and continues to expand today.

How do we know this? Edwin Hubble discovered that all distant galaxies are redshifted. Therefore, he reasoned, they must be moving away from us. Are we so unpopular that everyone is racing to get out of our neighborhood? No, it turns out that every galaxy is moving away from every other galaxy. Close galaxies are wandering away from us in no special hurry. But the farthest galaxies are racing away, whirling outward at unfathomable speeds. As time goes on, the amount of space between the galaxies increases because space itself is expanding.

Once astronomers observed that the universe was expanding, they realized that in the past the universe must have been much smaller than it is today. Calculations show that approximately 13.7 billion years ago, all the matter and energy in the

At the center of the Crab Nebula is a rapidly spinning neutron star (the small white dot at the center of the ringlike structure), which is generating a whirlwind of high-energy particles.

Alex is looking at a nearby spiral galaxy, one that is similar to the Milky Way Galaxy. He is pointing to the location of a supernova (which can't be seen in this photo) with the tip of a pen.

universe was packed together in an extremely hot and dense state.

Did the universe really begin almost 14 billion years ago? Some people are uncomfortable with the idea that the universe had a beginning. Yet astounding as it may seem, predictions based on the big bang theory have turned out to be true.

For example, scientists predicted that if the big bang actually happened, the entire universe should be bathed in a slight glow of radiation left over from that first stupendous explosion. They also predicted that this microwave radiation, coming from every direction in the universe, would be barely detectable, glowing at a frosty 3 degrees above *absolute zero*, the coldest possible temperature for any object. This glow, called the cosmic microwave background, was identified in 1965 by Arno Penzias and Robert Wilson, who received the Nobel Prize for their discovery.

If you'd like to see the big bang, you can—that is, if you get your television signal from an antenna and not from cable. Switch your dial to a position where you find static, or "snow," a salt-and-pepper pattern that fills the entire screen. One percent of the static you see comes from radiation produced in that first explosion long ago.

BIRTH ANNOUNCEMENT

If you don't like the name *big bang,* you're not alone. The astronomer who first used the term, Fred Hoyle, was actually making fun of the whole idea. Some people have always thought that the big bang should be renamed.

In 1993, *Sky and Telescope* magazine announced a contest to find a better name for the grand event that gave birth to our universe. The magazine received thirteen thousand entries from forty-one countries. Some of the names suggested were Super Seed, Hubble Bubble, and Bertha D. Universe. In the end, the judges, who included Carl Sagan and a well-known journalist named Timothy Ferris, decided to stick with the old name—the big bang.

Astronomers were also curious about the future of the expansion. If you throw a ball into the air, gravity pulls on it and brings it back down to Earth. Astronomers wondered if all the matter in the universe, along with its gravity, would slow the universe's expansion in the same way.

But how much would the universe slow down? Would the galaxies keep coasting outward forever? Would the expansion eventually stop? Would gravity cause the galaxies to fall back toward each other again?

By looking at the expansion history of the universe, astronomers hoped to learn more. The original goal of the High-Z Supernova Search Team was to measure how much the universe is slowing down. Theoretical astronomers had made predictions that depended on the observed amount of matter in the universe.

Look around. Everything you see is made of matter: your body, a grain of sand, and the stars in the sky. If the universe has lots of matter, gravity would have a strong pull and the universe would eventually collapse again. A

BELOW This illustration shows one possible history of the universe. On the left is the "big bang," the explosion that gave birth to our universe. The universe expands, and the galaxies move farther apart, until gravity takes over and the galaxies begin to contract or move toward each other again. In the end, they come together in a "big crunch." Since the discovery of dark energy, astronomers believe that the eventual contraction of the universe is unlikely.

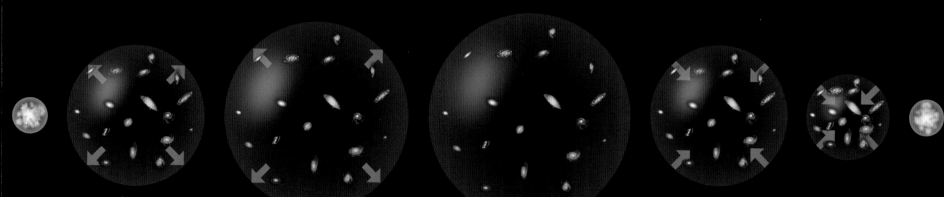

smaller amount of matter would mean that the expansion would slow down but keep going.

The astronomers knew there was also something called *dark matter* that would influence the results. Dark matter is not related to dark energy except that both are "dark," that is, neither emits light and neither can be seen through a telescope.

If dark matter can't be seen, then how do astronomers know it's there? It turns out that galaxies have more mass than meets the eye. Individual galaxies, swirling around a center, would have flown apart long ago if not for the gravity from invisible dark matter that holds them together.

Not much is known about this dark matter. Is it made of burned-out dwarf stars? Is it made of strange particles, such as *axions, squarks,* and *photinos*? All we really know is that in the regions of space visible with a telescope, scientists can detect approximately six to eight times more dark matter than ordinary matter.

But in spite of this extra matter, the High-Z Supernova Search Team got a surprising result. The expansion of the universe wasn't slowing down at all. In fact, it was going through a growth spurt!

"What we found was that in the last five billion years, the galaxies have been speeding up, not slowing down," says Alex. "It was the opposite of what we expected."

Adam Riess, a young researcher working with Alex on Brian Schmidt's High-Z Supernova Search Team compared nearby supernovae to distant ones and discovered that the distant supernovae were dimmer than they should be. This meant that all the galaxies, except those moving together in clusters or groups, were hurtling away from each other at greater and greater speed. In 1998, Alex's group and another team of astronomers led by Saul Perlmutter of the Lawrence Berkeley National Laboratory

This photo shows evidence of dark matter. The Hubble Space Telescope peered through the center of a huge galaxy cluster more than 2 billion light-years from Earth. The cluster plus the dark matter within it acts as a giant lens, bending and magnifying the light of more distant galaxies far behind it. Some of the distant galaxies are distorted by the "lens" and appear as wisps or curves of light. The faintest objects in this photo may be galaxies that are more than 13 billion light-years from Earth.

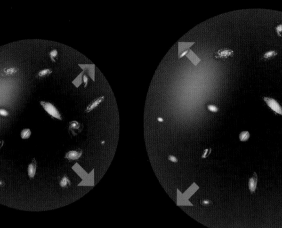

ABOVE Astronomers now believe that because of dark energy the universe will continue to expand and the galaxies will fly apart at faster and faster speeds.

announced these results to the world.

Now Alex and his team want to know more. Like detectives at a crime scene, they want to recreate the time line. Remember that astronomers look backward in time and see these objects as they were when the light left them, millions or billions of years ago. By measuring supernovae from different eras, astronomers can tell how fast the universe was expanding at different times in the past.

Imagine that you have a photo album with pictures from your grandfather's life. You have photos of Grandpa walking to school as a teenager. One photo shows Grandpa as a young adult riding a bike.

Later he got a van to accommodate his growing family. After he retired, he bought a hot little sports car. Now he's something of a racing fiend. Like the universe, Gramps is speeding up!

In the same way, astronomers can look back in time and put together a photo album of the universe's life. We can't see dark energy, but we can see the objects it's pushing. Supernovae give information about the motion of the galaxies over the entire course of the universe's history.

"We're asking ourselves: What was the universe doing one billion years ago? Two billion years ago? Three billion years ago? All the way up to eight billion years

ago," says Alex. "A detailed measurement of supernovae will help us find out why the universe is behaving the way it is."

Astronomers believe that dark energy is responsible for the acceleration. Albert Einstein, one of the world's greatest scientists, believed that "empty" space has its own special kind of energy, and many astronomers think that this is what is pushing the universe apart.

Early results indicate that for nine billion years, galaxies moved away from each other more and more slowly because gravity pulled at them and kept them from flying off. Then about five billion years ago, galaxies got far enough apart that gravity couldn't slow them down as much. Dark energy took over, giving all the galaxies an extra shove, pushing them away from one another faster and faster.

"A lot of people agree that this is now the number one problem in astrophysics: what is dark energy?" notes Alex. "There's dark energy everywhere. Every cubic inch of space has just the tiniest little bit of it. In fact, there's dark energy in this room. But compared to the air or gravity, there's not much."

Perhaps not much dark energy exists in a room. But the huge expanse of empty space that separates the galaxies contains vast quantities of this mysterious substance. Scientists now estimate this energy makes up 73 percent of the universe. And in the future, the amount of dark energy will continue to grow as the universe expands and the space between the galaxies increases.

What will happen if the speed of the expansion and the amount of dark energy keeps growing? Will the billions of bright galaxies fly away forever? Will they fade like sparks in the night? Perhaps tens of billions of years from now, the Milky Way Galaxy

Ryan and Alex are looking at a two-dimensional display of a supernova. This particular candidate supernova is too faint, and the spectrum of the night sky dominates. The spectrograph being used to obtain this spectrum is DEIMOS.

COMPOSITION OF THE UNIVERSE

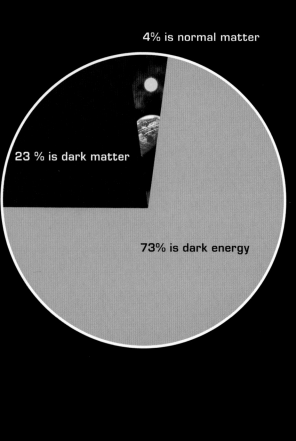

4% is normal matter

23 % is dark matter

73% is dark energy

may be all alone in the dark.

Remember, none of this will happen for tens of billions of years, long after the sun has stopped shining. Even so, some people, including scientists, find ideas like dark matter and dark energy very unsettling. Normal matter—the stuff of trees, animals, people, rocks, air, planets, gas, and stars—makes up only 4 percent of the universe. Strange as it may seem, 96 percent of the universe seems to be made of two ingredients that no one understands. What is dark matter? Nobody knows. What is dark energy? We know even less about that. Astronomers are really the ones in the dark.

THE KECK CONTROL ROOM (WAIMEA, HAWAII)

It's the second night back in the control room, and Alex has a problem. The spectrograph isn't working. The technician is trying to repair it, but nothing seems to help. Meanwhile, precious telescope time is being wasted.

"The guide camera is freezing up," says Alex. "This is really too bad, because the first part of the night is more important than the second half."

That's because the distant objects Alex wants to observe need to be high above the horizon. As Earth rotates, the objects move toward the horizon—just as the sun and moon do. Alex can't get a good reading if he has to view an object more than about halfway down to the horizon, through too much of Earth's atmosphere. The extra atmosphere will distort the image.

Suspense builds in the room as the moments tick away. After about an hour, Alex gets permission from Greg Wirth, the instrument scientist on duty, to work with a different spectrograph, the Deep Extragalactic Imaging Multi-Object Spectrograph (DEIMOS), a 20,000-pound device. DEIMOS can analyze the light from 130 different galaxies at one time. It's a lifesaver.

"This could help salvage part of the night," says Alex.

Now Alex and Ryan try to figure out how to work with this new instrument to get the results they want. They've lost a lot of time, and they decide to cut their original list of nine objects down to four. They'll keep the telescope on each object for forty minutes.

Alex decides what to observe, how long to observe, and what to look at next. Ryan's job is to take a "quick look" at each object. If the object seems promising, they might decide to do a longer exposure of it.

One problem is that light from the background sky and light from the galaxy can mix with light from the supernovae, creating a mishmash. Ryan subtracts the extra light and transforms the supernova's light into a spectrum. Once Ryan has a spectrum, he figures out the redshift of the entire galaxy.

Alex and Ryan have a spectrum on K402.

"There's something there, but it's really, really faint," explains Alex, obviously disappointed.

What have they found? Minutes go by as Ryan tries again. He types feverishly

RIGHT

Alex and Ryan look at a computer screen that allows Alex to control what the DEIMOS spectrograph is doing. To the right is the computer screen on which the resulting spectra are displayed.

ABOVE

This photo shows the death of a sunlike star. The star has shed its outer layers of gas and dust, and the central core has shrunk to a white dwarf (still visible as a glowing dot in the center). In about 5 billion years, our sun may come to a similar end.

at his workstation and finally produces another spectrum. A white dwarf about to explode as a Type Ia contains carbon and oxygen. When these elements start to fuse together, other elements—such as silicon, calcium, and iron—are produced.

"Yes!" says Alex. "It's a Type Ia supernova. WOW! We can see the calcium line, and the weak silicon line here."

But they've lost a lot of time and one object is all they managed to get.

"This is what happens sometimes," says Alex. "You have great weather, but the instrument isn't working. Sometimes the weather is bad or the wind is too high. You never know."

After midnight, the high redshift supernovae have moved out of range. Alex uses his telescope time to get the spectra of nearby supernovae. He wants to compare these nearby objects with the distant ones.

"We have to measure a bunch of them," says Alex. "This is definitely not the most important use of Keck. Much of this work can be done by slightly smaller telescopes. But we have to use our time efficiently."

A view of some of the six
telescope domes at the summit
of Mount Hamilton.

BLACK HOLES
BEHAVING BADLY

Mount Hamilton, California

Most of Alex's day-to-day observational work is done at the Lick Observatory, located at the summit of Mount Hamilton in California. The trip to the top follows a twisting road bordered by green meadows and oak trees. Six research-grade telescopes nestle in the hills at the summit. The visitor's center is open to the public throughout the week, and observatory guides give talks inside the dome, housing the historic 36-inch refractor telescope.

The Shane 120-inch (3-meter) reflector is the largest and most powerful telescope at the Lick Observatory.

But not all the bodies at Lick are the heavenly kind. James Lick, an early California settler who donated money for the observatory's construction, was buried there in 1887. Visitors on a private tour can view his tomb under the Lick telescope. It's marked by a vase of flowers and a brass tablet that reads: "Here lies the body of James Lick."

The visiting scientists who use the observatory are assigned rooms in one of three dormitories. Meals are served in the dining hall, and astronomers can order a special "night lunch," which includes a hot beverage in a thermos. Astronomers are night owls and they need their caffeine or hot chocolate.

Staff and visitors and their families share living space with the astronomers, and the dorms can get noisy during the day. One of the hardships of an astronomer's life is trying to sleep when a neighbor is moving furniture, banging suitcases, or trying to start the car. Luckily, the basement of the Shane telescope dome has a room with no windows, no telephone, no Internet connection, and no noise. It's perfect for Alex when he needs to sleep in silence after a hard night's work hunting supernovae.

This time, Alex has come to Lick with two research students to study nearby supernovae with the 120-inch (3-meter) Shane telescope, named for Donald Shane, a former director of Lick Observatory, who helped acquire funds for the telescope. But Alex is also here to monitor his robotic telescope, KAIT (Katzman Automatic Imaging Telescope). KAIT's mirror is only 30 inches in diameter, much smaller than Keck's.

"You might wonder why I'd be interested in such a small telescope," he comments. "But instead of needing an observer at the controls every night, the computer does the work. The computer knows what to observe, for how long, and how often."

KAIT can't compare with larger telescopes, such as the Blanco or the Keck, that can observe many more galaxies in a short period of time. But KAIT's strength is that it searches automatically, scanning seven hundred to thirteen hundred galaxies each night, depending on the season. (Summer nights are much shorter than winter nights.)

The telescope observes some galaxies more often than others—bright, nearby galaxies are monitored every other night. Alex sometimes refers to KAIT as his "supernova search engine."

It's important to catch a supernova at the beginning of its cycle. Type Ia supernovae reach their maximum brightness in about twenty days and then slowly become dimmer over the next eighteen months. By observing the entire light curve or history of brightening and fading, Alex can determine just how powerful each individual

Gamma-ray bursts (GRBs) are the most powerful explosions in the universe (except for the big bang). They occur about once per day and consist of brief, intense flashes of gamma radiation. The mission of the Swift satellite is to detect these bursts and alert astronomers on the ground so that they can study the bursts' afterglow.

supernova really is when it reaches its peak brightness.

"With this telescope, we find maybe two supernovae a week. They're rare," notes Alex.

KAIT has other uses as well. Alex is intrigued by a certain kind of supersize supernova, sometimes called a *hypernova*. He studies this second type of supernova for a very different reason. Hypernovae might help explain how bizarre objects known as black holes are created.

KAIT will drop everything if it gets a signal from the Swift satellite, an instrument that has been specially designed to detect *gamma-ray bursts* (GRBs). Swift can turn on a dime to find the location of these bursts, flashes of energy that appear from any direction in the sky and last anywhere from a fraction of a second to a minute. Hypernovae are thought to be the source of some of these gamma-ray bursts.

During the first minute after its explosion, a hypernova can emit a million times more energy than all the stars in the Milky Way Galaxy. If one went off near us, it would be as if millions of hydrogen bombs were exploding all over the planet. No one knows when or where the next hypernova will be discovered, but it's not likely to be close enough to threaten our planet.

"For decades, people didn't know what caused the gamma-ray bursts, partly because we couldn't tell exactly where they occurred," says Alex. "But the satellites have become more precise in locating them. When we find one, KAIT zips over to that part of the sky and starts taking pictures to try to find the vis-

SEEING THE LIGHT

You may not realize it, but you come equipped with two amazing radiation detectors. Your eyes are designed to receive a narrow band of electromagnetic radiation we call visible light.

Other forms of electromagnetic radiation are all around you. The *electromagnetic spectrum* is the name for all the different kinds of energy that travel through space in a wavelike pattern. Stars and other astronomical objects emit these waves that give astronomers information about the universe.

Electromagnetic waves have various degrees of energy—energy that's useful to people. For example, the sun's light can be gathered by solar panels and used to heat buildings and homes. X-rays can penetrate the soft parts of a body and take pictures of the bones inside.

In order of decreasing energy, electromagnetic radiation consists of: gamma rays, x-rays, ultraviolet rays, visible light, infrared radiation, microwaves, and radio waves.

Gamma rays are the most energetic kind of electromagnetic wave. On Earth, they are produced by radioactive atoms and nuclear explosions. Gamma rays can kill living cells and are sometimes used to treat cancer. But some gamma rays seem to come from the farthest edges of the universe and may have been produced by stars that exploded billions of years ago.

ible light that sometimes accompanies the gamma-ray burst. And we've found a few.

"There are actually two types of gamma-ray bursts. I'm studying these objects because one kind, the kind that lasts longer than two seconds, seems to be the link between some supernovae and black holes."

Gamma-ray bursts come from all directions in the sky and most arise from outside our galaxy. Now it appears that a number of them are beacons that signal the creation of some of the most mysterious objects in the universe, black holes.

Many people have heard of black holes—deep, bottomless wells from which nothing can escape. Science fiction movies show them as monstrous matter-sucking drains in space. It seems as though everyone is fascinated by these mysterious objects.

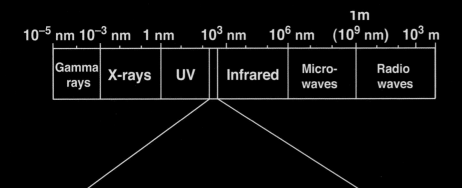

10^{-5} nm 10^{-3} nm 1 nm 10^3 nm 10^6 nm   (1m) (10^9 nm) 10^3 m

Gamma rays	X-rays	UV	Infrared	Micro- waves	Radio waves

Many objects in space emit a stream of energy (consisting of electric and magnetic fields) traveling in a wavelike pattern at the speed of light. The entire range of waves is called the electromagnetic spectrum.

A TICKING TIME BOMB

Eta Carinae is one of the most amazing objects in our galaxy. This gigantic star, which is four million times brighter than our sun, may be a huge powder keg about to explode as a supernova.

On Earth, large objects such as the Great Wall of China or Mount Everest tend to be solid, steady, and long-lasting. But enormous stars such as Eta Carinae are violent and unstable. They burn their nuclear fuel rapidly, shred their outer layers, and undergo dramatic outbursts. At times, Eta Carinae puts on a fireworks show, shooting out huge flares or blazing up in a sudden burst of brightness.

A giant cloud of gas and dust surrounds Eta Carinae and keeps it veiled in secrecy. Astronomers have never seen the star itself, which is 7,500 light-years from Earth. But recent observations in x-ray, radio, and infrared light indicate that Eta Carinae may actually consist of *two* stars.

Eta Carinae could continue "erupting" like a dangerous volcano until the day when it suddenly lets go in a frenzy of self-destruction. It could even end as a hypernova, outshining all the stars in the galaxy. Will this event occur tomorrow or in sixty thousand years? Nobody knows.

How would life on Earth be affected if Eta Carinae explodes? Astronauts in space might be harmed by a blast of deadly gamma rays coming from the star. But life on Earth would be shielded and protected by the upper atmosphere.

In recent years, Eta Carinae has brightened again. What will happen next? Astronomers can only watch and wait.

Gas and dust clouds surrounding Eta Carinae can be seen in this Hubble telescope image.

But a black hole is black. It can't be seen through a telescope. How can scientists study something that looks like nothing?

Hypernovae are part of the answer. Just before a star explodes as a hypernova, its core collapses to form a black hole. As the black hole rotates, a jet of radiation and particles shoots off into space. If by chance that jet is pointing in the direction of Earth, astronomers see a gamma-ray burst.

Astronomers have another way to locate black holes. These objects like to throw their weight around, and that makes it possible to detect them.

Some stars appear to have invisible companions. By analyzing the star's spectrum, astronomers see that it's being pulled one way and then another. First the spectrum is redshifted as the star moves away from Earth. Then it's blueshifted as it moves toward Earth. From changes in the spectrum, astronomers can figure out the mass of the object that's doing the tugging. If this unseen object is extremely massive, chances are good that it's a black hole. Why? Because astronomers don't know what else could be small and invisible and yet extremely massive.

"You take lots of spectra of the visible star," Alex explains. "And you'll see the normal star going toward you, then away, then toward you again. Blue, red, blue, red, blue, red. We rule out all the other possibilities of what the object could be."

Another way to tell if an object is a

This is an x-ray photo of material surrounding an object that is probably a black hole near the center of the Milky Way Galaxy. Jets of material are sometimes ejected from this object. The dull red clouds to the left and right are hot gases, remnants from past explosions.

This illustration shows a black hole orbiting a companion star. The black hole strips gas from its companion, channels it into a flat "accretion disk," and then blasts the material out in two opposite directions at a 90-degree angle to the disk.

HOW TO MAKE A MONSTER

You've probably seen lots of holes in your life: water holes, gopher holes, and keyholes. But you've never seen anything as weird as a black hole.

Black holes come in many sizes. Supermassive black holes are found at the center of galaxies and can have as much as a few billion times the mass of the sun. When we say that a black hole has mass, we don't mean that it is made out of solid material. The mass, or material, in a black hole has been squeezed to such an extent that it has actually vanished from the universe, leaving only its gravity behind.

A star-size black hole is born when a star at least twenty times the mass of the sun ends its life (in some cases) as a hypernova. The core of the star collapses, getting denser

and denser and smaller and smaller, until it becomes a point called a *singularity*.

At the singularity, both space and time stop. It's difficult to imagine a place where time does not pass and matter has no volume, but that's what happens at the singularity.

If you fell into a black hole, you wouldn't be sending postcards back home. As you approached the center of the hole, you would be ripped apart by gravity. In fact, if you fell feet first, the force on your feet would be so much stronger than the force on your head that you'd be pulled into long strands of spaghetti!

Even if you could survive, you'd have no way of getting a message to your friends back on Earth. The gravity of a black hole is so strong that nothing can escape its grip, not even light.

That's why no one has ever directly seen a black hole—and no one ever will.

A newborn black hole can send out two jets of energy. These jets actually come from an area outside the black hole. These are the bursts that the Swift satellite and KAIT detect. For every burst we do see, several hundred occur that scientists never see because the jets are pointed in a different direction, that is, away from Earth.

Black holes sound like something you'd find only in a science fiction story. But they are consistent with scientific theory, with the observations of astronomers, and with Einstein's equations. Most scientists believe that black holes really do exist.

black hole is to examine the material from a companion star that swirls around the black hole. Gas being sucked into a black hole from the companion doesn't plunge into it directly. It goes around the black hole in the same way water swirls down a drain. As it loses energy, the gas spirals closer and closer to the black hole. The intense gravity near the black hole causes the gas to get hotter and hotter until its temperature reaches 5.4 million degrees Fahrenheit (3 million degrees Celsius). At that temperature, the gas emits x-rays that can be detected.

"All that heated-up gas produces x-rays," says Alex. "And we optical astronomers say, 'Gee, there's a regular-looking star. But regular-looking stars don't produce x-rays, so this one deserves our attention.' What we're seeing is the companion star, not the black hole. Because they're so far away, they look like the same point."

Black holes are the most fascinating and mysterious objects in the sky, and Alex has helped find about six of them. Astronomers still have much to learn, though. How many black holes are there in the universe? Do black holes ever shrink? What happens at the singularity?

At the Lick Observatory, Alex uses the Shane telescope to follow up on the nearby supernovae that KAIT discovers. The Shane control room looks something like the cabin of a spaceship. Two monitors allow Alex and his students, Brandon Swift and Mohan Ganeshalingam, to take "quick looks" at the incoming data. A storm is brewing, and another monitor at the end of the room is currently tracking the weather, including the temperature, humidity, and wind speed.

The Kast Double-Beam Spectrograph, the

one Alex is using, is really two spectrographs, one that samples red light and one that samples blue light. These two spectrographs reveal the presence of different elements. The silicon line that helps identify a Type Ia supernova can be seen with the red spectrograph. But other identifying lines, such as one of the calcium lines, can be seen with the blue spectrograph.

"One thing we're interested in is just how diverse supernovae are," he says. "If they have differences in their peak power, those differences might show up in their spectra. That would be very useful to know."

If you want to learn about cheetahs, you might begin by looking for a big cat with spots. But leopards have spots too, so how do you tell them apart? You must look closer and note other differences between the two animals. It's helpful

The Shane control room. The telescope operator, Bernie Walp, makes some adjustments to the telescope from his computer workstation.

to know that cheetahs have more rounded spots. And a leopard hunts at night, while a cheetah hunts during the day. Knowing that fact may give you a hint about what kind of prey each of them hunts.

The more Alex learns about supernovae, the better he can draw conclusions about them, about the expansion history of the universe, and about the nature of dark energy. And changes in the overall pattern of acceleration can help astronomers explain dark energy. But that isn't the only reason Alex is interested in these amazing objects.

In the bellies of the stars, hydrogen and helium turn into new kinds of matter. The very elements in our bodies were forged in the furnace of stars that became supernovae. Without supernovae, there would be no planets, no buildings, and no living creatures on Earth.

If not for supernovae, we would know nothing about the extreme states of matter. Supernovae produce objects we would never encounter in our ordinary lives.

"Supernovae give rise to some of the most bizarre objects in the universe—neutron stars and black holes," says Alex. "We can't study these things in the laboratory because we can't make them on Earth."

As for star formation, supernovae may also play a part in that process. They may even help guide the evolution of life.

"When a star blows up, it sends a shock wave through the gas in a galaxy and that may trigger the formation of stars," says Alex. "Supernovae also generate cosmic rays that give rise to mutations

A technician, Bob Owen, examines the Kast Double-Beam Spectrograph.

The Shane, a reflecting telescope, has a mirror that weighs 4.5 tons and can focus light at three different locations along the length of the telescope. From 1959 to 1974, the Shane 120-inch (3-meter) telescope was the second-largest telescope in the world. Today it is used for a number of projects, including the search for extrasolar planets, that is, planets orbiting stars other than our sun.

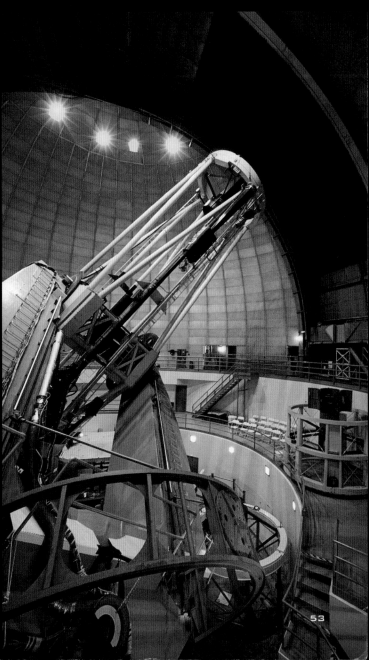

here on Earth. While most mutations are harmful, some cause new creatures to evolve. So in a way, supernovae help create new life."

The study of supernovae probably won't cure cancer or produce a better toothpaste. But Alex has the perfect answer when people ask him why it's important for scientists to study supernovae.

"Nothing is more important than something that led to our existence. When people want to know what's in it for us, I say, 'What's in it for us is us.' "

ABOVE This "starburst galaxy" is going through an explosion of star formation. Many of these new stars are very massive and bright. They use up their fuel quickly and explode as supernovae. A chain reaction of star formation and supernova explosions can spread through the center of the galaxy. In this photo, gas and debris are blasting outward at millions of miles an hour, spreading elements such as oxygen and carbon throughout the universe.

BIBLIOGRAPHY

Goldsmith, Donald. *The Runaway Universe: The Race to Find the Future of the Cosmos.* Cambridge, MA: Perseus Books, 2000.

Gribbin, John, and Mary Gribbin. *Stardust: Supernovae and Life—The Cosmic Connection.* New Haven: Yale University Press, 2001.

Katz, Jonathan I. *The Biggest Bangs: The Mystery of Gamma-Ray Bursts, the Most Violent Explosions in the Universe.* New York: Oxford University Press, 2002.

Kirshner, Robert P. *The Extravagant Universe: Exploding Stars, Dark Energy, and the Accelerating Cosmos.* Princeton: Princeton University Press, 2004.

Pasachoff, Jay M., and Alex Filippenko. *The Cosmos: Astronomy in the New Millennium,* 3rd ed. Pacific Grove, CA: Thomson Learning, 2004.

Rodarmor, William. "A Conversation with Alex Filippenko." California Monthly, June 1996.

Schilling, Grovert. *Flash! The Hunt for the Biggest Explosions in the Universe.* New York: Cambridge University Press, 2002

Wheeler, J. Craig. *Cosmic Catastrophes: Supernovae, Gamma-Ray Bursts, and Adventures in Hyperspace.* New York: Cambridge University Press, 2000.

RESOURCES FOR STUDENTS

Books of Interest

DK Publishing. *Stars and Supernovae.* New York: DK Adult, 2001.

Goldsmith, Donald. *Supernova! The Exploding Star of 1987.* New York: St. Martin's Press, 1989.

Jackson, Ellen. *Looking for Life in the Universe.* Boston: Houghton Mifflin, 2002.

Newton, David E. *Black Holes and Supernovae.* Brookfield, CT: Twenty-First Century Books, 1997.

Rau, Dana Meachen. *Black Holes (Our Solar System).* Minneapolis, MN: Compass Point Books, 2005.

Websites for Students

Ask an Astrophysicist
imagine.gsfc.nasa.gov/docs/ask_astro/ask_an_astronomer.html
An archive of frequently asked questions on a number of astronomical topics. The following are included: black holes, dark matter, supernovae, the Milky Way and other galaxies. For middle school and up. Plus a teacher's page.

Astronomy for Kids
www.frontiernet.net/~kidpower/astronomy.html
Information on the solar system, stars, galaxies, comets, and much more for elementary school students.

Imagine the Universe

imagine.gsfc.nasa.gov/docs/science/science.html

Basic information on black holes, dark matter, quasars, light curves, spectra, and gamma-ray astronomy.
For middle school and up.

WEBSITES FOR TEACHERS

Classifying Galaxies

www.smv.org/hastings/galaxy.htm

An interactive lesson for children in fifth to ninth grade. Information on spiral, barred spiral, elliptical, and
irregular galaxies.

Good Astronomy Activities on the World Wide Web

www.astrosociety.org/education/activities/astroacts.html

List of more than one hundred websites from the Astronomical Society of the Pacific, featuring astronomy activities
and resources for K–12 science classes.

Mauna Kea Observatories

www.ifa.hawaii.edu/mko/

Photo of the top of Mauna Kea. Click on a dome to visit various telescope websites.

Telescopes from the Ground Up

amazing-space.stsci.edu/resources/explorations/groundup/

The history of telescopes, background information on light, lenses, and telescopes, plus other tools for teachers.

CLUBS AND ORGANIZATIONS

Resources from SKY AND TELESCOPE

skyandtelescope.com/resources/

A site that will direct you to an astronomy club or organization in your town or area.

The Binocular Messier Club

www.astroleague.org/al/obsclubs/binomess/binomess.html

E-mail: ocentaurus@aol.com

Even if you don't have a telescope, you can join the Binocular Messier Club. For beginning observers and
experienced amateurs. All you need is a pair of binoculars and a membership in the Astronomical League.

Constellation Hunter Club

www.astroleague.org/al/obsclubs/consthunt/const.html

A forum for the novice observer to become more familiar with the constellations and brighter stars.
Must be a member of the Astronomical League.

HOW THIS BOOK WAS RESEARCHED

Ellen Jackson, the author, and Nic Bishop, the photographer, accompanied Alex Filippenko to Waimea, Big Island, Hawaii, where we watched Alex and Ryan Foley tune in to the universe in the Keck control room. We also joined Alex on his trip to the summit of Mauna Kea at 13,796 feet, where the working conditions for Nic were challenging. Laura Kinoshito, the Keck public information and outreach officer, came with us to the summit and was an invaluable resource. We enjoyed meeting members of the Keck maintenance crew, management staff, engineers, and telescope scientists.

We also visited with Alex at the Lick Observatory atop Mount Hamilton in California, where we met two of Alex's research students, Brandon Swift and Mohan Ganeshalingam, and several of his colleagues. All of them generously shared information about the telescope, the operating procedure, and the fine points of astronomy—and put up with a certain four-footed member of our party.

Alex is grateful for the love, support, and encouragement of his family. From the left are Alex's brother and sister-in-law, Ivan and Reka, Alex's mother, Alexandra, holding Leo, Alex's father, Vladimir, Alex, son Simon, daughter Zoe, wife Noelle, and daughter Caprielle.

ACKNOWLEDGMENTS

Many thanks to Alexandra Filippenko, and Leo. Without the two of you, this story would not have been told. I'm deeply grateful to Professor Joseph Miller, former director of Lick Observatory, who was extremely helpful at a critical time. Thanks, also, to the following people: Joel Aycock, Keith Baker, Ryan Foley, Mohan Ganeshalingam, Bill Healy, Grant Hill, Leslie Kissner, Sasha "Birdie" Newborn, Bob Owen, Robin Prehn, Tim Saloga, Barbara Shaeffer, Chuck Sorensen, Paul Stomski, Brandon Swift, and Bernie Walp.

Thanks to Hannah Rodgers. And a supernova-size thanks to our editor, Kate O'Sullivan, for her patience and kindness. She asked lots of hard questions and set a high standard for this book. I'm especially indebted to the following people who reviewed this manuscript: Vijaya Bodach, Ron Miller, Dr. Phil Plait, Carmel Robertson, Tanya Stone, Linda Urban, Carmella Van Vleet, and Steve Whitt.

GLOSSARY

absolute zero: The point at which a substance has no heat.

atoms: Tiny particles of a substance.

axions, squarks, and photinos: Subatomic particles that have not actually been detected but are predicted by some scientific theories.

big bang: A super-powerful explosion that scientists believe created the universe approximately 13.7 billion years ago.

black hole: Extremely dense invisible object that forms when a massive star collapses from its own gravity. Nothing inside a black hole can escape, not even light.

dark energy: An unexplained energy that is causing the universe to expand at a greater and greater rate.

dark matter: Material that doesn't emit light and that cannot be seen in the sky, even with a telescope.

Doppler effect: The variation in the frequency of sound or light waves that occurs as the velocity of the object and observer change relative to each other.

electromagnetic spectrum: The range of all wavelengths of electromagnetic energy that is made up of electric and magnetic fields. The spectrum includes gamma rays, x-rays, ultraviolet rays, visible and infrared light, microwaves, and radio waves.

element: A basic substance that can't be separated into other substances by ordinary chemical methods. Iron and gold are elements. Water is not because it can be separated into hydrogen and oxygen.

galaxy: A huge collection of stars, star clusters, dust, and gas that measures thousands of light-years across. Astronomers estimate that approximately 100 billion galaxies can be seen by the world's telescopes.

gamma-ray burst: An intense outburst of gamma rays that comes without warning from a random spot in the sky.

gravity: The force by which matter attracts and is attracted to other matter.

guide star: A bright star located near a dimmer object that astronomers want to observe through a telescope.

hypernova: An extremely powerful supernova thought to be the source of gamma-ray bursts that last longer than two seconds.

light curve: The brightness or intensity of light from an astronomical object that changes over time.

light-year: The distance light can travel in one year—5.8 trillion miles or 10 trillion kilometers.

mass: The amount of matter contained in an object.

Milky Way Galaxy: The collection of stars, dust, and gas that makes up the galaxy in which our sun is located. The Milky Way Galaxy contains more than 100 billion stars.

neutrons: Subatomic particles that have no electric charge and are found in the nuclei of atoms.

neutron star: The compressed core of a massive star that has exploded as a supernova. A neutron star is composed of densely packed neutrons.

photons: Particles of electromagnetic energy that travel through space at the speed of light.

redshift: A shift in electrical magnetic wavelengths toward the red end of the spectrum.

singularity: An infinitely small and extremely dense point at the center of a black hole where time and space stop.

spectrograph: An instrument that breaks light from an astronomical object into its different colors. This information allows astronomers to determine the temperature at a star or supernova's surface, the atoms that are present, and so on.

spectrum: The colors that can be seen when white light is split apart into its components. A rainbow is a natural spectrum.

standard candles: Objects that put out a known amount of energy. Astronomers can use the known power and measured brightness of these objects to calculate distances.

supernovae: Gigantic explosions that occur at the end of some stars' life cycles. The name comes from *super* (greater in quality, amount, or degree) and *nova* (something new). The word *nova* originally indicated an object that had brightened and appeared to be something new in the sky. *Supernova* is the singular form.

white dwarf: The remains of an old star (less than 1.4 times the mass of the sun) after its nuclear energy has been used up. A white dwarf is a small, faint, whitish star.

PHOTO CREDITS

NASA/CXC/ASU/J. Hester et al.: p. 22, 34–35

NASA/CXC/JHU/D. Strickland: p.53

NASA/CXC/MIT/F. K. Baganoff et al: p. 49

NASA/CXC/SAO: p. 4

NASA, ESA, Andrew Fruchter (STScI), and the ERO team (STScI + ST-ECF): p. 37

NASA, ESA, The Hubble Key Project Team, and The High-Z Supernova Search Team: p. 24

NASA, ESA, and K. Noll (STScI): p. 41

NASA/ESA/ASU/J. Hester & A. Loll: p. 22

NASA/ESA/JHU/R. Sankrit & W. Blair: p. 6

NASA, ESA, S. Beckwith (STScI) and the HUDF Team: p. 59

NASA/ESA/STScI/AURA/the Hubble Heritage Team: p. 53

NASA/HST/J. Morse/K. Davidson: p. 48

NASA/JPL-Caltech: p.4

NASA/JPL-Caltech/Univ. of AZ/C. Engelbracht: p. 53

NASA/JPL-Caltech/Univ. MN./R. Gehrz: p. 22

NASA/STScI: p. 4

All other photos by Nic Bishop

Illustrations below contain material credited as follows

NASA: pp. 23, 25, 32–33

NASA E/PO, Sonoma State University, Aurore Simonnet: p. 46

NASA, ESA and the Hubble Heritage Team (STScI/AURA): pp. 2, 8, 12, 13, 18–19, 36, 38

NASA/JPL-Caltech: p. 15

INDEX

Page numbers in *italics* indicate photographs.

This photo, taken by the Hubble Space Telescope, shows an endless sea of galaxies in a tiny patch of dark sky (less than one-tenth the diameter of the moon).